2

A Wisdom Guide & Journal

LOVE NOTES

from the Heart ~

Reflections to Encourage and Inspire You!

Linda S. Fitzgerald

with

JoAnn Corley

ISBN: 978-0615666020
ISBN: 0615666027

Printed in the United States of America

DEDICATION

LOVE NOTES is dedicated to women everywhere! Young, mid-life, 'vintage' and those very near the end of earthly life.

It's dedicated to women whose lives have touched ours in unspeakable ways. Women who have born significant loss and survived. Women who have made their mark on the world; and those whose world experiences their *mark* daily!

They are ordinary women leading extraordinary lives. Extraordinary women touching the ordinary and transforming it into the out-of-this-world!

Women who laugh with us from their soul & cry with us when life has thrown a curve ball & we struck out at home plate. Women who love us even at our worst!

Most of all, it's dedicated to the women in my life. My beautiful mature daughters and their daughters (and one son). And to my Momma from whom I learned that life isn't always fair; but it behooves me to play fair. And to my Dad who taught me how to love and that humor always makes the world a better place to be!

A special thanks to my collaborator and AWI friend, JoAnn Corley! Without your wisdom, JoAnn, this book would never have come to be!

INTRODUCTION

Books come from the heart of the author. Whether fiction or non, poetry or prose; the words we read come from the depths of the writer's soul!

This book is no different. It began as "Daily Doses" to the women who have become part of the 'fabric of my life'* at the Affiliated Women International™ online community, THE CONNECTION STATION™.

Over time, the collection of "doses" has grown to 800 – or more. They continue to come at least 5 times weekly - sometimes on Sunday.

LOVE NOTES is designed to be a "working journal"-- a book that provokes self-discovery. A book that makes you "think"! About life, about success, about relationships with family, friends and those in your community ~ and about love!

It is our hope that when you come to the end of the year with JoAnn and me that you will know yourself more fully; that you will have grown personally and professionally, and that you will have applied what you've learned to the next chapter or season of your life ~ with greater wisdom than before.

So come travel the road to your personal greatness with us. Read slowly, carefully and with deep intent. Ponder the "reflections" seriously. Then record your own reflections in order to deepen your self-wisdom and self-esteem!

Finally, open yourself to deeper and more significant relationships ~ treasuring each and every one in your heart ~

Linda & JoAnn

From Colleen's Desk. . .

I think you hit it out of the ballpark with this !☺

"Love Notes" reached the depths of my soul as it will any woman who simply wants to make a positive difference in the world. Linda and JoAnn have achieved a "slam dunk" with this simple—yet profound—food for thought gift!"

Colleen C. Barrett
President Emeritus, Southwest Airlines Co.
and Co-Author (with Ken Blanchard) of "LEAD WITH LUV"

Let The Journey Begin. . .

WEEK ONE: CHOOSE LIFE!

The old saying is that life begins at '40'! I say life begins when we decide to live it. Live it fulfilling our long-held dreams & visions.

If you're still waiting for it to begin; what are you waiting for?   Today is the day to start.

Don't waste another moment just thinking about it.

Do it _now_!

Warmly,

Linda

Reflections for Week One . . .

You know when people say, "Now this is living." What does that statement mean to you?

I've found if you don't define your own life, you will end up (particularly women) living the life other people want for you.

I feel the most alive when. . .

Are there elements in your life undermining the life you really want, if so – what are they and what will you do to change it?

Are you clear on how valuable your life really is?

What is it that you really want from your life vs. what you "think" you should want?

Your Reflections ~ Week One

WEEK TWO: CHOOSE LIFE!

"The story of the human race is the story of men and women selling themselves short." – Abraham Maslow

Abraham Maslow was a 20th century psychologist who studied human behavior and motivation. His seminal work, "The Hierarchy of Needs" stemmed from his desire to study those in society he considered "self-actualized"- those he believed had achieved the fullness of their destiny! He developed a pyramid of human behavior from our most basic needs to those he labeled "being needs".

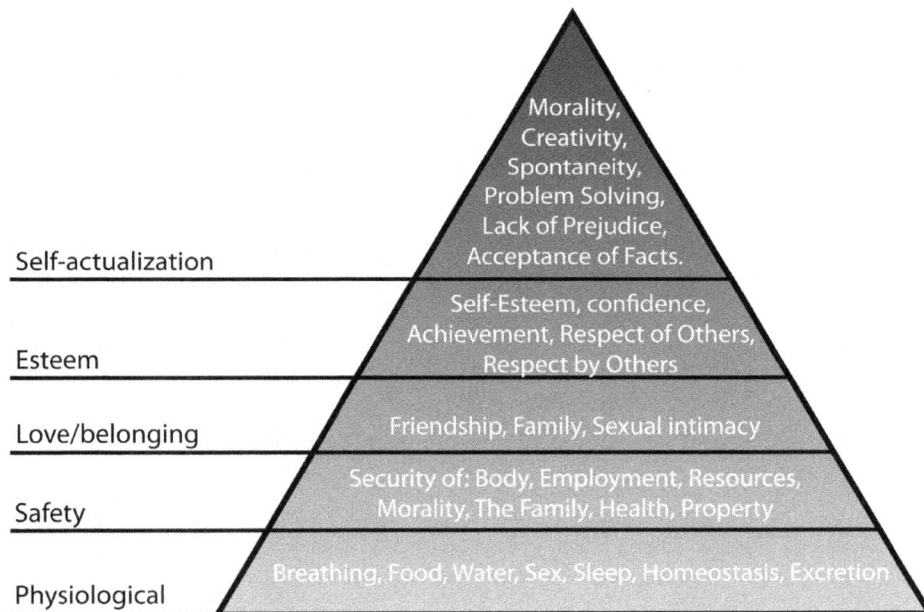

The sad commentary on Maslow's work is his discovery that, at any one-life season, only 1-2% of the population achieves "self-actualization".

Since we are talking about "life" and choosing it wisely; let me suggest that you place "self-actualization" on your "to-do" list. Choose today that you will pursue, with all diligence, the destiny that is yours!

Reflections for Week Two ~

All of you are meant to exist, and yet from birth on many things sabotage our full existence. With women, sometimes our need to belong, to fit and help, can sabotage our uniqueness.

Are there ways that you are compromising the real you?

Are there areas in your life you're avoiding that could afford you growth and thereby a greater emergence of "you"?

Is there any way in which fear is holding you back from being fully and completely you?

Your Reflections ~ Week Two

WEEK THREE: CHOOSE LIFE!

I don't normally do a "Love Note Sunday"; but today is different. So much rattling in my brain and heart that is knocking at the door of my mind and screaming. . . LET ME OUT!

It occurs to me that everything we need to achieve the destiny for which we are designed is never out of reach. In fact, it is so close to us that we rarely discover it without something knocking us for a loop!

It hides in the deepest recesses waiting to be discovered once we pick ourselves up; brush off the muck & mire and sit down to make sense of what life has just delivered.

The truth is; its hiding place is a location we rarely look. In fact, it's a door many never even discover; let alone open and explore!

Everything we need to achieve the destiny for which we are designed is right where it needs to be. . . WITHIN

Yes, <u>within</u> us all the time. In fact, we were born with it!

If you haven't unlocked that door; I encourage you to seek it out, insert the key into the lock, turn the knob ~ and open. . .

Reflections for Week Three ~

We live so much outside ourselves, particularly as women. Everything outside us is clamoring for our attention - family, work, laundry; and it all keeps our focus outward. Yet, in order to unlock the door we must attend to our inside so that the outside can operate better, with deeper meaning & satisfaction. All In all, "it's an inside job."

Time, for the inside is key! When will you set aside time for yourself – to nurture your inside?

What do you need to do to make that happen on a regular basis?

Where will you go and what will you do to attend to the inside of you?

Your Reflections ~ Week Three

WEEK FOUR: CHOOSE LIFE!

Earlier I repeated what we often hear – that "life begins at 40". If so, do we have to wait until age 40 to begin living? And just what is *"life"* anyway?

Maslow thought life was about becoming. Becoming all we are destined to be: growing into our full maturity & aspiring to a much higher level of *"life"* than most folks.

Let me just say this: Life is not about a particular chronological age. It's not about taking the easy road either. It's about embracing who we are and celebrating each and every facet of "us"! And that means changing our focus to explore inwardly. Exploring, discovering and, YES – embracing ourselves. Wrinkles, warts and all!

Now if that's a fact-according-to-Linda; then life is far more than *existing*. And it's much more than simply wandering through the days doing what we absolutely must before turning out the lights on the day.

So let me suggest (a bit strongly I might add) that we choose this day to begin <u>living</u>; that we choose to explore our many-splendored selves. That we determine it's okay to be who we are and certainly worth the energy and effort to celebrate ourselves. . . warts and wrinkles, as well as the beauty we find within!

Reflections for Week Four. . .

Is it possible that the compilation of our life is built by every singular choice made? I believe choices are the building blocks of our lives.

This is a great chance to examine your choice making — a critical exercise to creating the life you want and course correcting if need be.

Examine:

What choices you make daily in certain areas of your life...

Do those choices align with your values?

Do they get you the outcomes you really want?

Do you abdicate your choices to others and then complain about the outcomes?

How often do you use the phrase, "I have no choice."... oh yes, you do!

Your Reflections ~ Week Four . . .

WEEK FIVE: CHOOSE LIFE

We all know the story: Dorothy, the Tin Man, Lion, Scarecrow and the wicked witch. And of course, the Wizard - who isn't really blessed with magical powers at all. Or is he?

If you recall the story; he disappoints because he can't - or doesn't have the power to give each what they want by simply clicking his fingers. But he does have something else that is more magical than 'magic'.

What he has is *discernment*. An ability to see that each of the characters in "The Wizard of Oz" is endowed with the very thing they desire and long for. But he has another quality that is even more important. . .

He has the power to encourage. Not in any mysterious way; but by simply pointing out what is obvious to him. And that is encouragement. Not only does he discern the fact that the power for change resides within each; but he conjures up a magic dose of "Yes, Mr. Scarecrow, you have what it takes - now just do it!"

We have days when all we want is a magic potion that will transform the "now" into a future we long for. And we often think it's far out of reach -- out there someplace at the end of the "yellow brick road" or a rainbow.

Well it may well be. But it won't happen because we meet a wizard along the way.

The truth is, the "wizard" is <u>within</u> each of us. The ability to arrive at our desired destination is tucked inside. And it's been there all the time.

Follow the yellow brick road if you must. Search for magic potions if you think it will do the trick. But before you give up the journey; look <u>within</u>.

I tell you - "Ms. Empowered Woman, you have what it takes - now just do it!"

Reflections for Week Five . . .

As little girls, we were dreamers – dreamy eyed of future possibilities. In fact we probably used the phrase, "that is magical."

Then reality struck; the sparkly magical gave way to heartbreak realities. Yet, is it possible that in spite of all that, we can still create, be in, and decide to have magical lives everyday?

How would you define magical?

Is magical, perhaps, an interpretation of life that comprises gratitude & purpose combined with purity of heart and spirit?

If you've lost your magic, it's time to discover it again…create it for yourself and others…do the magic and be the magic.

Your Reflections ~ Week Five . . .

WEEK SIX: CHOOSE LIFE

To propel themselves forward, ducks must thrust their heads out first.

Let this be a week when you imitate ducks by sticking your head out first in order to move forward.

And remember, there's always a cheering section eager to spur you on as you gain new territory and stake your claim on life as you are meant to live it! You may not see them or even hear them. Just faithfully know they are there – for you!

Reflections for Week Six . . .

Sticking your head out means you've got to be assertive and there in lies the rub. Women, even in this day and age are socialized not to be assertive. For some of us, it might even feel down right unfeminine, rude or inappropriate.

Let's just say then that "sticking you head out" can be framed as simply taking initiative, taking a step forward, movement in a determined direction.

When you look at your life, what areas have you not done that?

What areas do you want to start doing that in?

In what ways?

And with whom?

Your Reflections for Week Six . . .

WEEK SEVEN: CHOOSE LIFE!

"Fear, get thee behind me!" That's the phrase for the week.

The journey to life – life lived to its fullest – is strewn with scary things. Scary words, scary actions – even scary people! But it doesn't have to be your 'lot' in life to give into the scary things that dog us daily.

So I say: "Let nothing that would engender 'fear' in you enter your path this week. Speak to it and simply say, "Fear get thee behind me!"

And 'swoosh' - it's gone!

Reflections for Week Seven . . .

Have you ever heard this, "Fear means fantasized event appearing real?" Fear, I believe is the enemy of human potential and the enemy of <u>your</u> destiny.

Are there areas of your life where fear has taken a hold?....held you back?

What can you do to take baby steps to overcome fear, in essence move past it — that's really all it takes — one choice, one decision at a time.

Your Reflections for Week Seven . . .

WEEK EIGHT: CHOOSE LIFE!

Life takes us on many journeys. Some are exhilarating; leaving us breathless but energized. Others are not so exciting. They drag us to the pit and we wish we could hide our heads until they pass.

I say, stay the course! "Pit life" will not last forever. Before long, that which dropped us down a long dark shaft, will give way to joy and laughter.

So stay the course. Don't hide among the muck. Lift up your head and look for the light. And before long, it will shine through the darkness showing the way out of the "pit".

Reflections for Week Eight . . .

Managing the "pits" is truly a life success skill. Sometimes we may have even said, "This is the pits."

And yet the pits can be very useful. The pit in car racing is for refueling, getting new tires, attending to needs.

Would you be willing to reframe how you see the pits in your life?

How can you use them differently?

What can your pits teach you about yourself, your needs, others in your life?

What can or have you learned about your previous pits?

Your Reflections for Week Eight . . .

WEEK 9: CHOOSE LIFE!

No one likes them! Bullies that is. And for some time now, *bullying* has been a national conversation as such behavior is having dire consequences in too many cases.

Yet, it goes on all the time! If we're truly honest with ourselves, we'll admit that we're all very good at it.

Now before you rise up in arms that I would dare suggest that any of us engage in such gross behavior; let me briefly explain!

While we would never think of or even consider bullying another person; we don't hesitate to do it to <u>ourselves</u>. Yes, we engage in mental gyrations that if expressed openly about another would be labeled "*bullying*".

Yet we think nothing of mentally (and sometimes emotionally) berating ourselves. In the psychological world; we call that "*old scripts*".

So as we prepare to "**choose life**" and to live it to the full, let's declare a moratorium on "*bullying*". And let's begin with us. Let's choose to erase such self-defeating thoughts from our minds.

May take a while to totally accomplish; but hey, it's a start!

Reflections for Week Nine. . .

Though bullying is destructive behavior, there is a strong energy around it. It gets noticed – it causes things to happen. How about this – let's take the energy used for negative and direct it towards good – good thoughts, empowering thoughts, actions toward change.

How can you turn around the negative energy into constructive energy?

In what areas can you channel that energy of "I don't like that" into let's do something about it?

Can you develop the life skill of taking that energy and re-directing it into fueling your will and harnessing desire to construct different outcomes?

Your Reflections for Week Nine . . .

WEEK 10: CHOOSE LIFE!

Seems like a good week to choose a new path in life! Not an intention to scrap all that has gone before; but a week to take into account what has fallen into place. And then move from that point to a path that opens new doors to personal discovery!

May I suggest that for this week, you choose to take a giant leap forward.

Take tall strides and walk quickly over anything in your path --anything that holds you back…anything that mentally keeps you from the appointed goals for the week.

For the choice to live life to the full is about trusting and leaping. I think of it like the scene in *"Indiana Jones & The Last Crusade"* when to get to the location of the Grail; Indiana must have faith to step into what appears to be a huge crevice on the path! If you've seen the film; you know exactly what I mean!

If I may be so bold, let me recommend you take the kind of high jumps it takes to overcome any obstacles that would keep you from your appointed destination. Whatever it is; choose this week, to put them in the dust behind you.

I believe it's high time you did so! How about you?

Reflections for Week Ten . . .

Can <u>you</u> be bold?

Are you willing to be bold?

In what areas of your life could you use or demonstrate a dose of boldness?

Are times of boldness necessary for a fulfilling life – to fulfill <u>your</u> life destiny?

Are you willing to take the leap and trust yourself and your destiny to grow your wings on the way down?

Your Reflections for Week Ten . . .

WEEK 11: CHOOSE LIFE!

Life is hardly about perfection! Even the experts get it wrong from time to time.

Even the "experts" get it wrong from time to time!

Standing on the deck at a Wyndham resort a few weeks ago, I admired the landscaping. How perfect the edging is. How seemingly perfectly shaped the bushes & shrubs. Since I love good landscaping; I marveled at how different that which was done by "experts" appears to my 'novice-done' at home.

Being the observer of life and events that I am, I fixated on 2 small growths wedged in behind large bushes that shielded them from the sun. They were obviously too close for comfortable growth. Most of all they looked totally out of place in that location.

The following occurred to me. . .

"Even the experts get it wrong from time to time!" Yes they do. Although that doesn't take away from their expertise; it does bring them down somewhat to the level of us 'mere mortals'.

So my advice (and wisdom) for the week is to remember that <u>everyone</u> has an area of expertise. <u>You</u> <u>do</u> - I do. In reality, we <u>ALL</u> do!

But sometimes we error in our expertise and have to make course corrections. If that's how life is for you, then always take with you this thought . . . you may get it wrong from time to time; but it doesn't change the realty that you are an "**expert**".

It just means that you; me (ALL of us) are 'mere mortals'. And you know what?

I gladly accept that fact and actually revel in it. Hope you can do the same. . .

One thing for sure, we are the experts of our own lives! Though for women, because we are so relational, we sometimes abdicate that in certain situations to others.

Do you believe you are the source of understanding what's best for you? You are the expert of yourself?

Getting it right is all in the testing - the taking of risks. When that happens, we get informed.

Are you reading your life?

Are you letting all the experiences of life instruct you to learn more about yourself?

Are you trusting that? Seeing those lessons as valid?

How are you doing so?

Your Reflections on Week 11 . . .

WEEK 12: CHOOSE LIFE!

There are many things that go into making a successful life. Good strategies & planning, quality decision-making, wise choices, etc.

But the most important ingredient - the one we often leave out, is **confidence** in ourselves. Honest assessment of our skills, abilities, intellect, energy & wisdom.

And a dogged determination that we have what it takes. For all things considered; without belief in who we are and what we bring to the strategy and plans, we are bound to fall short and miss the mark.

Go forth this week, knowing you have what it takes. For I'm here to say - "**You Do!**"

And choose to march to the beat of your own drum & dance to the cadence of your heart's desire. When you do; you've chosen "life" and made the wise decision to live it fully. And adopted the determination to achieve the destiny for which you were designed.

Now that's what I call 'choosing life'!

Reflections for Week 12 . . .

I saw a quote that said, "Be yourself, everyone else is taken." The key is: do you really know yourself in practical ways? For example if you were asked, "What are the 3 qualities that describe you best?" Could you answer?

In a career setting – it's essential you are able to know and articulate your skills even better than the people interviewing you!

Are you clear about your skills and capabilities?

Will you take the time to compile the answers to that question?

Do you feel comfortable sharing those – expressing them – advocating them as you navigate your work life?

Your Reflections Week 12 . . .

WEEK 13: CHOOSE LIFE!

When you reach this "week", it may be the season for "pill-pushing". Colds, flu, general aches & pains. Depression that often sets in after a major life event (holidays, graduations, marriage, child leaving the nest).

Well this week, I'm pushing something vastly different. I'm "pushing" enthusiasm, energy, excitement, a positive mindset & optimism!

Here's how to take this "med":

1). Pop one or two of the above upon awaking; wash down with a smile.

2) Take another one or two at lunch and enjoy with a favorite food & friend.

3). Take one or two more during the evening as needed.

I guarantee you'll recover from anything that ails you in no time flat!

Oh, and keep this "med" handy as you may need to repeat usage on a regular basis. And rest assured; there are absolutely no *negative* side-effects!

Have an awesome week with a few of these wonder pills rattling in your pocket!

Reflections for Week 13 . . .

For sure we need constant "doses" of things that fuel us, keep our self-esteem in tact. As Les Brown once said, "You can't give out of an empty wagon."

Are you clear on the things – the activities that feed you – that fuel your spirit? (Remember this is unique for you – won't be the same for everyone.)

Do you have a list handy so that on "those" days; it can be your 'go-to' resource for self care?

Do you believe that spiritual health impacts physical health?

What will be your plan to maintain your "dose" level?

Your Reflections Week 13 . . .

WEEK 14: CHOOSE SUCCESS!

Most folks define "SUCCESS" in $$$ and cents. And the more of that stuff one has, the more the world judges' one a success.

But I say that success is not just how much money one has in her portfolio. No "success" can only be defined by YOU. You and you alone know what makes you feel (and be) successful.

Furthermore, what's in your "life portfolio" will be meaningful to no one else but YOU! Only YOU know what has meaning for you! And what is most valuable in life. . .

Never let the world define the word for you. No one else in the whole wide world can 'successfully' do that for you.

Thus I suggest that this week, take quiet moments to discover what's really meaningful to you. Then from that – formulate your very own "SUCCESS" statement.

Once you have it – POST IT on your wall. On your bathroom mirror and the refrigerator. Everywhere you'll see it upon arising and the last thing you'll see before falling asleep.

And I just suspect that one day you'll awaken to find that SUCCESS has arrived at the door of your life!

Reflections for Week 14 . . .

So how would you define success?

Have you been hesitated to put it out there because it's so different from the common definition?

Are you willing to own <u>your</u> own definition of success?

Do you think a definition might evolve over time and need to be refined and revisited?

Your Reflections Week 14 . . .

WEEK 15: CHOOSE SUCCESS!

Sometime ago, I posted a comment at Facebook about "richness"…that when we pursue riches, they seem to elude us. But when we turn our focus elsewhere; they often show up at our feet!

The truth is that each of us is "rich" in our own way. That is if we get over our addiction to and obsession for defining "rich" in terms of $$$ and cents.

As you go about the week; stop just long enough to recognize the ways in which you are "rich". If you have a way with words that bring comfort, encouragement and support to others - you were "born with a silver spoon in your mouth" (and on your lips!). Things like that! All the ways that you are blessed to have your needs met.

Most of all, stop and recognize the ways in which you are endowed to meet the needs of others.

Bottom line (as they say in the business sector): You **are** <u>RICH</u>! Enjoy it; celebrate it and then share some of your riches with others.

Reflections for Week 15. . .

Just like success, we do need our own definition of rich.

So what does being rich mean to you?

Do your life decisions reflect that definition?

Does your attitude towards challenges in your life reflect it?

How are you rich?

Do you have a "rich" list?

What would be the value in having one?

Your Reflections for Week 15 . . .

WEEK 16: CHOOSE SUCCESS!

Persevere! That's what it takes in life to arrive on the journey called "SUCCESS!"

And take someone with you who will "hold your feet to the fire"...that someone who knows how to persevere. That someone who knows how to motivate, cajole and spur you!

And take those in your circle of friends with you as well. They have a stake in your SUCCESS. They believe in YOU! And guess what? So do I and so does everyone reading this book.

With that kind of "fire", you can't lose!

No way around it – perseverance has to be developed. Nope, there is not a perseverance fairy god mother to just bestow you with it.

It's a life skill muscle, and like all muscles, needs to be exercised! The only catch - you have to be in a situation in which the exercising can occur. Ghez!

Are you willing to grow your perseverance muscle?

Are you willing to experience the pain of growth?

Have there been situations in your life when you avoided the opportunity to grow this muscle?

What can you do now to develop it?

Your Reflections Week 16 . . .

WEEK 17: CHOOSE SUCCESS!

SUCCESS is a journey - not a destination! Don't remember who said that, but it's wisdom.

So today, think of those who share your passion for life. Your passion for becoming all you are meant to be; your desire to achieve specific life goals; your hope that SUCCESS will 'dog' you every step of the way.

Single them out. Let them know you'd like them to travel the journey with you.

My suspicion is they'll be delighted you asked. And that with each new step you take; they'll be cheering and applauding.

So take the 1st step onto the road of SUCCESS. And know that you are not alone as you travel!

Reflections for Week 17. . .

Do you have "passion partners". . .they are a special lot. Just being around them, supercharges your desired and capabilities.

I've worked in both formal and informal partnerships and collaborations where I am much more with than without.

Who are those folks in your life?

Do you have passion partners in the areas of life that matter most to you?

If you don't have any yet — what will you do to seek them out?

Do you believe that having passion partners in your life can make a difference to your destiny fulfillment and happiness?

Your Reflections Week 17 . . .

WEEK 18: CHOOSE SUCCESS!

"Words" can make a dramatic difference in how we view ourselves as we progress on the path to SUCCESS!

Let us speak only words of encouragement to each other this week and be empowered as we let them sink deep into our hearts!

Listen! There's much love being spoken about <u>YOU</u> this week! May I suggest that you share those words with others in your life who can use a little of the encouragement and empowerment you are getting daily?

Reflections for Week 18. . .

Words create reality.

Do you believe that if you are more deliberate in your word usage, your life would feel and be different?

What words would you like to eliminate in your life?

What words would you like to add to your life?

Are you willing to stand up for "your words" with those around you?

Your Reflections Week 18 . . .

WEEK 19: CHOOSE SUCCESS!

Speaking of "words" as we did last week, the following occurs to me: "Let the Words you hear be one's that cause your spirit to soar! Soar with enthusiasm, energy & eager anticipation for what the future holds!

Then sit back - relax and prepare for the awesome journey that lies before you! A journey that holds the fulfillment of all you hope for and dream of. A journey that holds the fulfillment of your destiny design!

Reflections for Week 19. . .

Wow…just think…what you listen to - what you let into your mind will influence your subconscious and ultimately how you engage in life.

Would you be willing to do a "listening audit?"

What are you listening to now that you might need to change?

What do you want to add to your listening repertoire to help you get more of the life outcomes you desire?

What are you listening to inside yourself that you no longer want to listen to?

Your Reflections on Week 19 . . .

WEEK 20: CHOOSE SUCCESS!

Waiting on our SUCCESS to arrive is a virtue -- the virtue of <u>patience</u>!

But first we must do all that is humanly possible to make it happen. Nothing comes by magic or wishing it to be. It takes the companion of doing and waiting – waiting and doing – to bring about our desired outcome.

Ah, the rhythm of life - doing and waiting! Waiting and doing. . .

Let this be the week you get into the flow…into the rhythm…into the virtue of working as hard as you can – then acquiring the patience required to let it happen in its right time!

Reflections for Week 20. . .

Patience

You know, generally, people who are doers hate waiting! Additionally, patience reminds us of our humanness in creating results. It also suggests there are other elements in play that are necessary for outcomes to occur – we just can't see them.

Do you believe that faith is a component of being patient?

So, to increase our ability to wait, do we need to nurture and strengthen our faith and beliefs?

What does that mean for you personally?

What do you believe about other elements in play to assist you with your desires & dreams?

How deeply do you believe?

Do you need to develop more supporting beliefs that aid you in being patient?

Your Reflections on Week 20 . . .

WEEK 21: CHOOSE SUCCESS!

The way to *maximize* our market is to maximize "us". Bring all our heart & mind to the "project".

Hone every skill and ability. Put every ounce of energy into the process!

For our success begins and ends with "us".

So this week, take the first steps to *maximize*. In fact, set a plan in motion that will *maximize* a bit more each day.

And before long, we'll join you to celebrate the awesome results of your efforts!

Have an awesome *maximizing* week. . .

Maximize can be seen as realizing potential and that means going beyond where we're at currently and that means going beyond what's <u>safe</u>, <u>known</u>, or <u>comfortable</u>.

Are you willing to go beyond?

Are you willing to "get comfortable with feeling uncomfortable?"

Are you willing to dip your toe into the unknown?

What will you do to move yourself beyond?

Are the opportunities right now that can allow you to move out of safe and comfortable?

How will you leverage them?

Your Reflections Week 21 . . .

WEEK 22: CHOOSE SUCCESS!

Seems like yesterday we were eagerly expecting the start of a new year – even a new decade. We were enthused & eager to make the year better than the last – the new decade better than the last. After all, starting the next 10 years in a new century deserved a rush to pursue every possibility that lay before us.

With that in our remembrance bank; let me leave you with one word for the week - PURSUE!

Pursue the plans you made not so long ago as one year slipped into the next. As one decade slipped into the next, pursue personal growth. You know that thing about looking deep within using binoculars & trifocals if necessary. That exercise in which we discover the best that is us and polish that which is a bit tarnished. And most importantly, brush off the rust from those great skills you've been hiding in your 'closet'!

For the truth is – there is no better road to professional success than that which travels over our personal paths.

So this week, pursue that which appears to be the most viable approach to bringing out the best in you. And add a bit of spice by sprinkling into the mix that which will bring about your desired professional outcome!

But more than anything else - PURSUE! You have what it takes to <u>pursue</u>, <u>persevere</u> & <u>achieve</u>!

And don't let anyone tell you differently!

Reflections for Week 22 . . .

Pursue, go after, drive - does that describe you? It better if you want to get what you want!

Think about the areas of your life and the statements that you've made about what you want.

How bad do you want them?

Do you really want them or are they things you think you should want?

What are you willing to do to get them?

Are you willing to experience pain to get them?

Your Reflections on Week 22 . . .

WEEK 23: CHOOSE SUCCESS!

There's an old adage that we usually quit just before our ship sails into port. That success is just around the corner; but out of sight. And if we can't see it; we rarely have the faith that such is true; and the determination to wait it out.

This is true for most folks, so lest you think I'm pointing fingers - not so. I too am often short-sighted & faith/determination wanes as the waiting goes on and on and on. . .

But my NOTE for each of you this week is "**don't stop now**". I do believe it's darkest before the dawn. That success only eludes us because we give up too soon. I believe that we have what it takes to wait it out, full of hope and faith in the promises we've been given.

So today - take a page out of hero's pages. Sit down & rest if you must; but <u>don't</u> give up. Keep plugging away. Before long you'll see the long sleek bow of your "ship" rounding the corner of life's lagoon. And it will be headed straight for your dock!

Reflections for Week 23 . . .

On the journey of success, it's important to make the distinction between stopping and giving up. Sometimes we're tempted to give up because we actually need to stop — for a moment. We need to take a pit stop, get refueling for the upcoming blocks to the corner.

So, give yourself permission to stop — to stop for a purpose.

In what ways have you not stopped when you should have, so the greater destination can be reached?

Are there times when you don't give yourself permission to stop?

What are some constructive ways you can stop?

How will you use your "stopping" most effectively?

Your Reflections on Week 23 . . .

WEEK 24: CHOOSE SUCCESS!

Last week, I addressed the habit we often have of quitting about the time our success is coming around the corner. Some things take time and sometimes much longer than we want.

Something interesting about us humans - we want what we want; and we want it NOW! Yet it is rare that we get what we want NOW. Most often we must wait. And learn the art of PATIENCE which is not an easy art form to acquire.

If you're somewhat on the 'ragged edge' and thinking of giving up. . . let me suggest the following:. Give in to that feeling without actually carrying through. Take a break - it's okay! Walk away from whatever it is you so strongly desire and have worked so hard - for so long to achieve. Turn your attention elsewhere.

There's an old and famous saying that I paraphrase: commit your desires to PAPA; do all you can do as a woman - then wait. And if the w-a-i-t-i-n-g has gone on too long; then take a break! Don't give up; but give in to letting divinity work where us humans have no business interfering!

Did you know that walking away is a success strategy? Yep, in fact leaving something alone can many times reveal the truth of it.

So, in the spirit of stopping, you may need to add to it – letting go.

In what areas might you need to use this strategy?

What do you want to discover in doing so?

What do you want to get clarified?

In what area of your life do you want to gain more motivation?

Do you understand the distinction between letting go and giving up?

Your Reflections on Week 24 . . .

WEEK 25: CHOOSE SUCCESS!

I've been thinking about "timing", and how it fits into "choosing success"! You know what I mean - how great things come to us, but the timing is all wrong!

What occurs to me as I think about the entire aspect of timing; is that we often confuse an idea and timing. If a great idea we have doesn't produce the outcome we desire or at least think it should; we assume it was a "bad" idea!

The reality is there may be nothing wrong with the idea. What may be off in our thinking is the "timing". And that confusion can end up costing us big *time* over our lives.

So remember: "To everything there is a season". In modern translation, I believe that's wisdom telling us that a grand idea's "season" has yet to come. And in my book; "season" translates to "timing!"

Don't scrap that great idea just yet. Let it simmer & percolate until you think it can't simmer or percolate any more. That may just be the *time* when the "timing" is just right. . .

We must believe in timing and one of the best ways to get grounded in timing is seeing how it's worked in our lives and the lives of others.

How has the universal act of <u>timing</u> worked in your life in the past?

In the lives of others?

Would collecting timing stories from others, help strengthen your belief, acceptance, and understanding of it?

What can you do to embrace timing as your success partner?

Do you see timing as an essential success partner?

Your Reflections on Week 25 . . .

WEEK 26: CHOOSE SUCCESS!

Oh a week for a refreshing --a week to step back from pursuit & take time for reflection.

"Reflection!" Yep, you'll hear me say that a lot; but nothing is more important in life and the pursuit of our own definition of success than stepping back regularly to "reflect"!

It's also time to determine if or how far we might have traveled from the "basics". Whatever we desire; however we define "success" for ourselves, we began with a basic set of core values out of which our beliefs flow.

A sense of what we wanted as the ultimate outcome. In the rush to achieve, we often get very far afield.

This week, let me encourage us to review, reflect & assess.

1). Are we sticking to our basic set of core values and beliefs?

2).Have we traveled well beyond the boundaries of our original passion and purpose?

3). Do we need to run back to where we started & set the record straight about who we are and what it is we intend to do?

If so, then together, let's get back to the basics - for it is at that "basic" point our true success will begin to take shape and form.

I guarantee it!

Reflections for Week 26 . . .

One of the many definitions of reflection is one that suggests a return back. Part of reflection is the boomerang effect. It's instructive in that it lets us know what we're doing. It reflects back the results of decisions, choices- knowledge . . . a whole host of things.

Do you believe that using reflection in this way is essential to life success?

What has your reflection taught you about you?

What does your life results suggest about your strengths, your weaknesses?

Your Reflections Week 26 . . .

WEEK 27: CHOOSE RELATIONSHIPS ~

Family, Friends & Community!

"No man is an island, a person undo his own!" Well known saying that's just as applicable for women as for men.

None of us is alone in life. It may feel like it at times; but in reality, there's no truth to the feeling! We all have others about us and those with whom we are especially close - like family and lifelong friends. Our communication may be sparse and spotty at times; but when the chips are down – they're there for us!

Then there are those about us we don't even know. Folks we meet online in social networking sites. Folks we have yet to meet face-to-face.

The truth is that relationships are one of life's most precious (and priceless) possessions. Not that we possess the folks with whom we relate; but that we possess the privilege of being close with folks who mean the most to us.

So this week, step back from the busi-ness and chatter that comprises your days. Take time to count the ways you are blessed with priceless relationships. Write them down. Record how they are important to you.

And finally, take a moment to send each of them a note of appreciation, love and support!

One of the gifts of a relationship is what it can teach us about ourselves. If we say, "Hey that person is really bothering me," we are blaming the person for the bother. Instead use the bother as instructive. Instead ask, "Why am I bothered?"

Not only make a list of those who are priceless, but add to your list what you have learned.

…what have they taught me about me?

…how would I be different if this person was not in my life?

…are there other people I consider not so special who taught me things about myself?

Your Reflections Week 27 . . .

WEEK 28: CHOOSE RELATIONSHIPS ~

Family, Friends & Community!

Did you know that someone is thinking of you today? Someone who wants nothing but the best for you? Someone you may never have met personally; but knows who you are and what you bring to their life!

This week I want you to savor the knowledge that someone is thinking about you. When the chips seem to have fallen on unfavorable ground; remember that someone who cares is thinking about you. Someone who is thinking supportive thoughts sent across the universe. Sent with the intent to land in your mental synapses. Sent to 'snap' you out of a somber mood!

Consider it a mental greeting card with the following verse:

"Just to let you know you are being thought of today!

Thoughts of support for you in all you do!"

Keep this in mind as you plow through another week of life and living!

Reflections for Week 28 . . .

The fact that I can become mindful at any moment that someone cares, is thinking of me, has my best interest at heart - is powerful.

The second power is to return the favor, not only mentally, but physically.

Considering sending a "thinking of you" card - written in your own hand, with your spirit spilling through the pen and onto the pages...

Who needs a card like that?

What do you want to say that you've been saying in your head and heart?

What other ways can you tangibly express – "I've been thinking of you!"

Your Reflections Week 28 . . .

WEEK 29: CHOOSE RELATIONSHIPS ~

Family, Friends & Community!

"Let's stay connected!" A very important person in my life once spoke those words to me. They had significance and great meaning!

Connections are the 'stuff' out of which great relationships grow. And great relationships are the 'stuff' that keeps our heads above water when we hit the 'rapids'.

But great relationships can lead to something much more than "heads-above-water". They can lead to a sense of 'community' with others who share our values, our beliefs, our goals and sense of life purpose.

So this week, take a moment to ponder the "great relationships" in your life. Mentally call them up. Look them over carefully; turning them over and around to take in every valuable facet of the persons and the connections!

And as you do, may the mental fondling of those priceless relationships bring you calm seas all week long!

"Connecting is community – connecting is family."

Our society has changed so much, and a changed society offers us the challenge of redefining community and family. Sometimes, connection is thicker than blood.

How has your experience of family changed?

Do you want to define it differently?

How does connecting play into that?

Who do you consider is really part of your community - your family?

Your Reflections Week 29 . . .

WEEK 30: CHOOSE RELATIONSHIPS ~
Family, Friends & Community

Be a lightning rod! Be the brightest crayon in the box! Be a <u>connector</u>!

Of course, each of you already is a lightning rod for great new ideas & strategies. And you certainly are the "brightest crayon in the box". And I suspect you are more than just ample at making connections. Connections that mutually matter!

For great connections produce outstanding possibilities. Whether those awesome connections are with family, friends or in the community-at-large; they have amazing potential to enrich, encourage and empower all who experience the same sense of connected-ness!

This week, connect yourself with others who share the same awesome qualities. You know – "lightning rod sparks of enthusiasm"! Those who are as *bright a crayon* in the box as you are!

For together, you can make a vital and credible difference - if only in your corner of the world!

Reflections for Week 30 . . .

A lightening rod is awfully powerful. It brings a surge of energy that illuminates the sky. We have moments and time periods when we could use a super charge. An area of our life is not clear and we need some illumination on or about . . .

Who are the people in your life that are your <u>illuminators</u>?

Who are those who can <u>supercharge</u> you just by being around them or hearing their voice on the phone?

How can you be that for others?

Is there anyone in your life right now that needs a charge or an experience of illumination?

What do you need to do to make that happen?

Your Reflections Week 30 . . .

WEEK 31: CHOOSE RELATIONSHIPS ~

Friends, Family and Community

What more can we ask than to have peace, comfort, joy and a measure of success as we define it for ourselves? There isn't much more that can bring us a deep sense of satisfaction as we travel this journey called "life"!

Oh my I almost left out the most important thing we can ask for! ...the loving care and support of family and friends; relationships that last a lifetime and add more meaning and value to each day than we can ever express in words.

So today, determine to ask for that which will bring warmth to your heart & will enrich your spirit. Then when it comes; determine to give it away to another desperately in need of such "what more can we ask" woman. You'll find that both of you are filled to the brim with more than you ever hoped for or imagined!

You know sometimes we just hate to ask. The need is great but the ego is greater and to ask would mean scooping up a humongous spoon of humility. And yet, many times asking is the only way to get…after all not every loved one is a mind reader.

What are some needs you have that you've not asked for help?

In what ways have your ego stopped you from asking?

Have you every turned down help… knowing you needed it?

Are you willing to allow others to serve <u>you</u>?

Who are the people in your life who would love to meet a need you have, but have yet to make that request?

Is fear perhaps holding you back and if so, in what ways?

Your Reflections Week 31 . . .

WEEK 32: CHOOSE RELATIONSHIPS ~

Family, Friends and Community

Just think what we could do if money were no object! Or time was totally our own to control? Just think how successful we might be if there were no personal challenges to overcome and no one standing in our way!

What if I said it's possible to rid out lives and careers of many things we consider impediments to getting where we want to go – and be!

What if you could stretch marketing dollars because others were exercising "word of mouth" on your behalf? And how awesome might it be if "sisters" who share a mutual care, concern and respect for each other helped to stretch your time & energy. Women who care enough to send you the very best they find in and from their circles of influence!

Not possible you say? Well what if I said – "yes, tis' true!" Because it's a fact that others care about you – about your goals – about your deepest passions and desires – your SUCCESS!

So as you go about the next week, harbor in your heart the fact – the knowledge – that others do care. Then reach out & connect until you find them; build a friendship and then move together in mutual "lockstep" to get to where each of you want to be!

Ah I hear the stampede now. . .

Reflections for Week 32 . . .

It comes with the package you know - a friend or business connection for us as women, goes beyond just hanging out and occupying time together.

We love sharing — we love offering the resources at our disposal to support each other's journey. Consider the vast resources of . . . who they know, their natural talents, their passion for something, their ability to generate ideas . . . and many other resources we can't see or are even aware of ~

How will you harvest these resources?

What do you need that these resources could meet?

Are you willing to explore how to use these resources?

Do you really believe they are part of the "gift package" of a friendship . . . ready to be opened up at any time?

Your Reflections Week 32 . . .

WEEK 33: CHOOSE RELATIONSHIPS ~

Family, Friends and Community

There's a famous story about a woman with a critical need. She'd had the need for years. When she heard a man was coming to her area that she thought could help her; she rushed to meet him. But the crowd was so large & the press of those around her prevented her from getting as close as she wanted.

But she was undaunted! In some strange fashion, she was able to press forward and with outstretched arms, lightly touch the bottom of his cloak as he stood in the midst of the crowd.

That touch brought confidence and the resolution of her need in an instant. And her perseverance caught his attention. Not only did the illness from which she had suffered for so many years simply go away; but she was recognized and introduced to all for pushing against the odds.

Many times, all it takes for us to find resolution to the things in life that keep us from achieving, is to reach out & touch. Reach out and touch those who can help us. And in so doing, we are seen and recognized for who we are - and what we bring to the world.

May I suggest that this week, we reach out & touch! And let our touch be the source of recognition we need to take us from the crowd - to a place where we stand undaunted in the face of any impossible odds!

The power of touch – in so many contexts - is just amazing! The funny thing is - it's just a simple touch that can do so much.

A simple act of power can send a charge of energy to the person receiving and the person giving; like in a random act of kindness for example.

Do you believe there is **power** in *your* touch?

How can you touch someone spiritually, emotionally, mentally, and spiritually?

Do you take for granted the power of your touch?

How can you touch someone else and also empower yourself?

Your Reflections Week 33 . . .

WEEK 34: CHOOSE RELATIONSHIPS ~

Family, Friends and Community

RELATIONSHIPS: Those who know me well know of my adoration for the British tenor, Russell Watson. Not just because he has the most incredible voice, is lovely "eye-candy"; but because of his return to health & vocal strength after a serious brush with death!

At Christmas time, I gave myself a present. I purchased the download of the DVD recorded at Russell's Royal Albert Hall performance earlier this year. Yesterday I took time out to watch to the end.

In one of his delightful conversations with the huge audience, he noted what is important to him now that he's recovered. "Not houses, fancy cars or flashy clothes", he said. But "people and relationships!"

He noted that it's the people in his life and the close relationships that have the greatest value to him. The audience erupted in applause & Russell's eyes glistened with tears.

At special times of the year, perhaps more than others, our hearts & minds turn to "people and relationships". As a 'vintage' woman, I know the truth in his words. In the end, it all comes down to the people in our lives who support & care. The people whose candor helps us grow. Relationships that build us up without glossing over our growing edges!

My desire and hope for each of us this week, is that we'll take what our hearts & minds focus on at holiday seasons for more than just one season of the year. That we'll take it in our hearts and minds every day for each season and year of our lives!

Reflections for Week 34 . . .

Sometime holidays can be pretty challenging for a variety of reasons and usually that challenge centers around issues with "people." Holidays are times when people are missed, and some who will never come back. And yet, it doesn't mean we can't carry them, their spirit; the gifts they gave us — all the time. They may be physically gone, but the gifts of the relationship have not. Our heart is a wonderful house full of love, warmth, and memories.

What is your relationship to the holidays and people?

Are there gifts given from times and people in the past that you'd like to reclaim to hold and cherish in the house of your heart?

Who have been your special gift givers?

What are some fond memories that are truly gifts you can carry in your heart? Qualities of special people that have blessed you?

Your Reflections Week 34 . . .

WEEK 35: CHOOSE RELATIONSHIPS ~

Family, Friends & Community

Early yesterday I shut down my laptop and headed downstairs to await the arrival of my youngest granddaughter, Audra. Our plan for the day?...bake cookies and share lunch together. It was a day we had planned for weeks. I shopped to make certain all ingredients were on hand; set them out on the counter tops and even cleaned the oven. All was in readiness.

It was a great day of fun and celebration - one I will cherish all year through until time to do so again this time next year. In the quiet of evening, I reflected on how fortunate I am to have a nearly 11 year-old who wanted to spend time with her 'vintage' grandma!

To my utter amazement, the Master Card ad flashed across the TV screen. You know the one that ends with "Priceless". Yes, that was the word for yesterday. For the time Audra and I spent together.

But it is also the word for each person with whom I share life (that of course includes each of you!). So as we rush about today getting all in readiness, I ponder the following . . . "What are the most precious things in your lives?"

As evening falls wherever you are; may I encourage you to take time to ponder that which is "priceless" to you!

Wouldn't it be fun to create your own MasterCard commercial? What a fun kitchen table activity to do with family and friends.

Let's begin to create your own commercial . . .

Who is in it?

What do you say?

Where are you creating it?...and with whom?

How could you use this idea to promote the value of gratitude with those around you?

Your Reflections Week 35 . . .

WEEK 36: CHOOSE RELATIONSHIPS ~

Family, Friends & Community

"I lift up my eyes to the hills from whence comes my help!"

Some versions say "strength". Either way, this is one of my favorite lines from the Psalms. David, anointed King, had more adversity in his early years than most of us will encounter in a lifetime. He was hunted with the intent of being killed. He was reduced to hiding in dark, dank caves. At times, he was near to giving up on life - and on his appointed destiny.

Last evening I was struck by the final scenes in the classic TV series, "Criminal Minds". It was a father giving his young son permission to "let go". The words that struck me went something like this: "Sometimes son, giving in is winning!"

Many of us go through life seasons where we want to "give up". Giving up ought <u>never</u> be our strategy. Even when there appears no light at the end of a long, long tunnel.

But learning to "look up"; "wait for the strength that will come" and "giving over or in" is, at times, the only winning strategy. To do so, takes courage, hope and patience.

This week, if all you have left is an ability to "look up"; then do so!

If all that seems inevitable is to "give over or in"; then let that be the lay of the land now.

My bet is you will find it's the best winning strategy you will ever choose.

What do you have to lose?

Sometimes when life's challenges occur, it's all about how we name it – what we tell ourselves about the situation.

For example is "giving in – giving up?" Maybe yes...maybe no. Perhaps navigating life's challenges is more about the story we give something than the challenge itself. Sometimes we do have to "look up <u>and</u> give it up." <u>Surrender</u> is a powerful distress tool leading to life success.

What has happened that you need to give a new, fresh story about?

Is there something that's been looming that you really want to surrender?

What might be stopping you?

Do you need to do more looking up?

Can you make the distinction between "giving up" and "giving it up?"

Your Reflections Week 36 . . .

WEEK 37: CHOOSE RELATIONSHIPS ~

Family, Friends & Community

Everyone talks about it; but is anyone really doing it?

Community that is! Is anyone really engaging in the somewhat arduous work of building relationships around common interests, goals, needs or simply for sheer joy that 'community' brings to our lives?

Without a sense of community somewhere in our lives, with folks we trust and with whom we share life's most significant moments – life can be relatively bland. And that's putting it mildly.

This week, as you go about your daily chores – doing and achieving; give some thought to the "communities" of which you are a part. If you can't point to more than 1 or 2; be a doer and start one of your own!

There are communities by default and communities by choice. I believe to live a more empowered life - to fulfill our destiny - we need to engage in more communities by choice.

Examine your interests! (Remember our segment on passion partners?)

What new communities do you want to connect with?

What communities might it be time to disengage from? (yes...this is necessary as well – some only serve us for a time and sometimes we need to determine when that time has run out.)

What communities will help you grow?

Your Reflections Week 37 . . .

WEEK 38: CHOOSE RELATIONSHIPS ~

Family, Friends & Community

"You've Got A Friend!" is the title of a great James Taylor song from *my day*. The beauty of it lies in lyrics that state the obvious. That having a friend is one of life's most precious and valuable possessions.

We often underestimate the value of friendship while in our younger years. And we take it for granted until something unforeseen happens to end the relationship. Then the realization of what we've lost sets in to haunt us over time.

Funny thing, but us humans are made for _relationship_. Not just <u>any</u> relationship. Nor just vicarious acquaintances either. We're constructed to actually '*need*' the presence of others in our lives – a presence that goes deep into our souls, and remains.

Yes [blood] family is vital. But friendship has a vitality that no other relationship on earth can duplicate. And the loss of same through death, separation, disagreement or serious falling-out leaves a hole in our hearts that little, but time, can repair!

As you go about the week; remember that *you've got friends*. Do something special for them – and for yourself as well!

Sometimes friendships are so good and close, we might take them for granted. How about considering how much more rich and satisfying they could be if nurtured. Time is short.

Are those who are special — your "soul friends" aware of how much you really care?

Do you want to more actively nurture those friendships?

In what ways could you do that?

What friendships do you have right now the need a [serious] nurture boost?

Your Reflections Week 38 . . .

WEEK 39: CHOOSE RELATIONSHIPS ~

Family, Friends & Community

Last week, I shared some thoughts on having a friend – or friends. How human beings are made for relationship and the vitality that friendships bring to life.

This week, I want to say something about "family" -- those folks with whom we are connected by blood relationship or marriage to someone who is 'kin' to us by blood.

As I sit to write about "family", I find a strange silence. No thought or even the spark of a synapse firing. Why would the subject of "family" be so difficult to muse upon? After all, family is considered our prime human relationship. Isn't it?

Or is it?

Family can be difficult. It's expected that we will be close to those who share our blood lineage or have married into it. Yet sometimes just the opposite is true. And many folks have a hard time equating "family" with anyone who doesn't share our familial lineage!

I'm reminded of the time I was asked "how many grandchildren do you have?" To which I responded -"Six!" The person asking the question was amazed that I had "so many". She should have stopped while she was ahead; but went on to add that each of my 3 daughters must have 2 children a piece.

"No", I said. "I have three biological grandchildren and three via marriage", I happily reported.

The woman quickly sought to correct by assuring me that I had only 3 actual grandchildren since those acquired by marriage weren't *of my blood!* I was incensed by her insensitivity and narrow frame of reference! To me, blood lineage doesn't matter. The fact that two of my daughter's acquired daughter's via marriage gave me additional 'grandchildren'.

Now I see why "family" can be difficult to write about!...and even more difficult to define; often more so to relate to and exceedingly difficult to manage when worldviews collide.

So let me just leave you with this piece of wisdom gained over time. Yes, family is technically those to whom we are related by blood lineage or those who married into our blood lineage (or us into theirs!). However, in reality, *family is however we define the word for ourselves.*

And that's all that needs be said on the subject!

Reflections for Week 39 . . .

Do you need to release yourself from the traditional view and definition of family?

How has holding onto that perhaps not served you well?

How do you want to redefine family for yourself?

Who really is your family?

Who do you really want to be in your family?

Your Reflections Week 39 . . .

WEEK 40: CHOOSE LOVE

Ah yes, that beautiful word "LOVE". So rich in meaning; so complicated in expression and so often misinterpreted by those of us who seek it most!

There are a number of different understandings of the word LOVE and a number of different definitions as well. There's "romantic love" – you know that thing called 'chemistry' that attracts us to another and causes the blood pressure to rise; hormones to charge & a silly grin to cross our face at the mention of the other's name. It's the love that overtakes us in our youth, but sadly seems to fade as the years go by.

Then there's familial love. The love we have for family members, close friends and others who have considerable significance in our lives; but for whom the love we share is not "romantic".

And of course, the greatest form of LOVE is agape. The unconditional love we equate with PAPA for His children (us). The love that rises well above the romantic stage and says "I will love you no matter what!"

The love we have for our children and grandchildren. I recall that I could never have gotten the same understanding from my Momma had I engaged in some of the same behaviors growing up, as my daughter's did! Funny how agape grows along with the arrival of grandchild!

But LOVE is as St. Paul says "the greatest of these is love!" There are many worthwhile things in life: charity or compassion and care for others; faith in that which is bigger than you and me; hope that the indomitable human spirit will rise above all else in life. And then there is <u>love</u> & Paul says it is the "greatest" of all worthwhile things in life.

Let us commit ourselves to love! Let us commit ourselves to the pursuit of unconditional love. Let us commit each day to love the unlovely and unlovable. Let us commit to love that which once we thought had no worth or value. Let us commit to love with our whole heart, mind, body and soul.

Impossible? Perhaps.

But then perhaps not!

Reflections for Week 40 . . .

This is an essential topic of exploration because it is the foundation of every area of our lives. So work this section carefully:

What is love to you?

How do you define love?

Do you feel comfortable with loving yourself?

How have you demonstrated it?

Do you believe that loving yourself is essential to a happy life and successful relationships?

Would you like more love in your life?

Do you feel you are responsible to create more love in your life vs. someone else doing it for you?

Your Reflections Week 40 . . .

WEEK 41: CHOOSE LOVE ~ To Trust

LOVE involves an element of trust.

It involves trusting our emotions; our 'soul' to others - learning to trust others that invites them to love us in return.

Sally Hogshead, in the "*Fascination Matrix*" states the following: "Trust requires repeated exposure".

In other words, coming to "trust" others requires predictability. I come to trust others because I've spent time with them over the long haul and found them to be person's with whom I can 'trust' myself; my life, my business – my being. I can predict with considerable accuracy how they will be and respond.

We all know that trust between individuals, as well as individuals and brands, takes time. But in a world that spins faster & faster; few folks really want to take the time to gain mutual trust.

If LOVE has meaning and value to you, then give *trusting* a try. If trust is valuable to you; determine to take the time to get to know others. And don't hide yourself from them. Give them the time and opportunity to get to *know* you.

The outcome will be a lifetime of valuable relationships that are mutually rewarding - and beneficial! It may also be a LOVE you never thought possible!

Dating is a wonderful thing in that it affords the opportunity to reveal in stages. Those incremental revelations release trust, which is the glue of connecting.

Particularly as women, we sometimes empty the entire glue bottle prematurely. So applying wisdom in trust can build solid, abiding love.

With whom would you like to increase your trust?

Is there trust that needs to be repaired?

How have you worked with trust?

Do you feel the need to grow in the ability to trust?

Would it be helpful to have a "trust strategy"?

Your Reflections Week 41 . . .

WEEK 42: CHOOSE LOVE ~

"How much do I love you. . .let me count the ways!" - a line from a very famous poem.

This short "note" is just to say that counting the ways we are loved, supported and encouraged can put a smile on our faces and a spring to our steps!

And additionally it will do the same when we let others know how much they are loved, supported and encouraged.

Pick up the abacus of LOVE and count the ways. Then count the ways your love puts smiles on faces and springs to steps. Make it a week that counts for LOVE - one to remember always!

Reflections for Week 42 . . .

Is it possible that love is taken for granted — both in giving and receiving?

How have you been loved in obvious ways? . . .in less obvious ways?

Do you know that different people have different love languages?

Are there times when you've discounted how you've been loved by someone?

Are there people in your life where it would be beneficial to change how you express love to them?

Who would you like to say this to . . ."Thank you for all the ways you love me"?

Your Reflections Week 42 . . .

WEEK 43: CHOOSE LOVE ~

I believe in the miracle of LOVE ~ to heal hurts; to wipe away tears, to turn sorrows into joy!

Most of all, I believe in <u>YOU</u>! - each of you who are reading this "note" today. I believe that you have all it takes to become the woman you want to be – the woman you are **destined** to be.

That's LOVE!

Love acting through faith and confident assurance. Love inspiring and encouraging. Love speaking truth where only lies may have resided before! Love giving a nudge where complacency may have lain for a lifetime. Love acting bravely to speak that which until now was silent!

Yes, love in the form of words designed to heal hurts; wipe away tears and turn sorrow into joy.

Walk in that LOVE all week through!

Love is not only an emotion, but an action…

How can you put your love in action today?

With whom?

What love acts do you enjoy doing the most?

Do you have a love in action repertoire?

Does it need to be expanded?

Your Reflections Week 43 . . .

WEEK 44: CHOOSE LOVE ~

It has been said that "love is a many-splendored thing".

Actually it's not a "thing", but an invisible bond that brings 2 or more folks together in inexplicable ways. And it's less about emotion than about a decision.

This week, in the midst of a world seemingly a bit 'crazed', let's learn to love one another. A love that weeps when we are sad, laughs at our paltry jokes & defends each other no matter what.

For in so doing, each of us will become the woman we know we are. The woman we are when love wraps us in its warmth & protects us from that which would tear us apart.

Let's begin by telling someone who lives in our heart - "I love you!" I'll start. . .

I may never know you personally or have the privilege of meeting you face to face; but nevertheless, I love each of you!

I respect who you are as a woman; as a professional; as someone whose friendship increases me.

I feel honored that you are reading this "note" today, ready to put it into action in your own lives and that of others. For each of you make me more of who I am designed and destined to be!

Let us choose a love that builds up and does not tear down.

Let us choose a love that brings joy and rarely pain.

Let us choose a love that shows up just when needed.

And a love that knows no limits or bounds.

Let us choose a love that increases each other!

Reflections for Week 44 . . .

In essence YOU ARE LOVE! How beautiful and special is that!

Take that in for the moment . . . if more people realized that – how would the world be different?

How would relationships be different?

How would the energy of your life be different?

Who else in your life could use that understanding about themselves?

Your Reflections Week 44 . . .

WEEK 45: CHOOSE LOVE ~

Love is about much. And it is about much we rarely consider "love" or "loving acts!"

Often times the loving thing we can do for others is to "open doors" on their behalf. And more times than not, we are unaware we've done so until later - when they tell us.

The reality is that most often, we never know it or even take second notice that we've done anything of significance!

Over the years, I've come to learn that *opening doors* for others has an upside for me as well. It may not have motivated me to do so; but the results play out to the mutual benefit of us all.

Love is funny that way. The more you give it away to others; the more it returns again. Like a boomerang, returning time and time again!

So this week, let's look for special opportunities to *"open doors"*. Doors that revolve & swing both ways! Doors that have the word "LOVE" emblazed on both sides in bright & colorful letters!

Have an awesome week going through *doors* that hold considerable promise for us all.

Love really is about opening…opening up ourselves, opening up others because of the way we are with them, opening up potential and opportunities . . .

What does your love need to open . . .

A conversation

A wound for healing

A new community

A new project

A fresh approach for forgiveness

Love is a powerful opener ~

Your Reflections Week 45 . . .

WEEK 46: CHOOSE LOVE ~

Last week, I spoke of giving the gift of an *"open door"* to others. Discovering an opportunity for someone and offering it as our gift. The gift of LOVE defined as 'connection' and 'opportunity'.

Then there are those times when doors open for us. A gift from PAPA regardless of how we define it. Albeit at the hands of another human being who knows that LOVE resides within!

My encouragement this week is to be diligent in watching for a door that swings widely open to admit you as you approach. I pray LOVE will keep you from passing it by without notice – thus missing what it holds for you.

I desire that it be a Gift far greater than you could ever have hoped for or imagined.

Reflections for Week 46 . . .

"Hey . . . I want to be loved this way . . ." . . . have you ever said that to yourself? If we are narrow in how we expect to be loved – might we miss all the ways we are loved?

What are some ways you've been loved that you may not have defined it as such?

Do you believe that you can be loved in a certain situation, though it may not feel that way at the moment?

Can you make a list from your life experience of ways you were loved, but didn't recognize it at the time?

Why would that be a good exercise?

Would that expand your life-love experience?

Your Reflections Week 46 . . .

WEEK 47: CHOOSE LOVE ~

RECIPE FOR THE WEEK:

Walk tall!

Be brave!

Find that which delights your soul.

Celebrate small things that bring a smile.

Be glad for those you LOVE!

Be grateful for those who LOVE you!

Add joy to the life of others

Let joy enter your life without fear or trepidation

Mix all together. Bake in a warm heart with fuel from your soul.

Enjoy every morsel and keep coming back for more – time and time again!

Reflections for Week 47 . . .

What's *your* recipe for the week? – Write your own and enjoy!

Your Reflections Week 47 . . .

WEEK 48: CHOOSE LOVE ~

LOVE speaks:

"Let the week dawn with enthusiasm & eagerness. Let it unfold with determination and persistence. Let it be a week when all you hope for, desire and dream of begins to appear over the horizon!"

Then let the planet hear our shouts as you each take your rightful place on the world's stage!

Do you believe that you deserve love?

*Do you believe that loving yourself and loving others should have an element of **boldness** to it?*

Do you live your love – out loud?

How can you do that more?

What can you do to take your rightful place as an act of love for yourself and others?

Where can you express your love – enthusiasm & eagerness even more?

Your Reflections Week 48 . . .

WEEK 49: CHOOSE LOVE ~

The greatest good we can do is often the least thought to be so. We stoop to help another pick up dropped packages when no one else seems to notice.

We hold the door for the fellow exiting behind us rather than let it slam in his face.

We stop to say a kind word to a friend whose demeanor says "it's not a good day!"

To make a difference does not have to be earth-shattering. It has only to make a difference to another.

A difference that lightens her load or eases his pain. A difference that in the grand scheme of things goes relatively unnoticed.

Never mind that few will ever know of our goodness as we walk the path to greatness. The point is that _we_ know it. . . and so do those for whom it was done.

Be a woman making a difference! Be a woman of LOVE. It fits you well. . .

Reflections for Week 49 . . .

Do you believe that loving in the little things has great value?

Here's a twist – do you believe that sometimes not acting is also an act of love?

Are there areas where a desire to love is actually creating the opposite effect?

This week is another opportunity to expand how you see love – in action or not....

What are some "little" acts of lover that you can do this week?

Where are some areas in which you might need to hold back a bit?

Your Reflections Week 49 . . .

WEEK 50: CHOOSE LOVE ~

LOVE comes in different sizes, shapes, demeanors & decisions. It sometimes comes in words that in another context would seem anything but 'loving'!

Some 1st days of the week are tough! After 2 days change of pace and focus; the return to weekly business, career chores or home management can cause us to grit our teeth and pull the covers over our heads.

The other side of the 1st day of the week morning muddle is the excitement of 40 + more hours to make things happen. Time to move closer to our desired outcomes.

For many of us it's at least 60 or more hours to weave minor successes into the tapestry that represents our individual achievements.

So as you pull on your "big girl pants" for the week; remember that perception is reality. And you have control over how you perceive the 1st day of the week to be.

The choice is up to you!

Determine that you'll yank on those britches; grab and gulp the last swig of coffee as you head out the door.

And put on your broadest smile – the one that everyone LOVES to greet. The one that says, "I'm on top of the world!"

Well if not the world; at least a new week. So choose to greet this 1st day of a new week filled with amazing anticipation and great expectations. That's the LOVING thing to do. .

.

Reflections for Week 50 . . .

I love the beginning of a new week. It offers up the power of new!

Love yourself in a way that you can take advantage of that power. The power of new is leaving the past in last week, forgiving yourself and others for failings and starting fresh.

How will you love yourself in this way this week?

How will you love others in this way?

To which areas of your life can you apply this?

Or in what areas does it need to be applied?

How can you use the power of new to keep your love fresh in all areas of your life?

Your Reflections Week 50 . . .

WEEK 51: CHOOSE LOVE ~

Be A REVOLUTIONARY!

Bold title. **Bold** suggestion!

Bold form of **LOVE**!

We tend to think of *"revolution"* as something negative. And often such actions have a negative impact on folks. On entire nations in fact!

But this week, I'm thinking of the word in a totally different context.

I'm thinking of us all walking out to the 'cutting' edge to boldly launch new dramatically positive things. I'm envisioning banding together for the good.

Yes, I'm suggesting a band of LOVERS not content with the status quo! A band of LOVERS who will step out on that ledge of uncertainty with fierce determination – for no other reason than it's the LOVING thing to do!

Let me say that we are a "revolutionary" – a "revolutionary" when we bring fresh new & bold ideas to our corner of the world. To those just waiting for our arrival. To those hungering & thirsting for our boldness.

It is when this happens that we LOVINGLY "revolutionize" for the betterment of all.

Never thought of it that way?

Well let me suggest a turn of thought. Be so **bold** as to put on the walking shoes of a *revolutionary*. Step out on the edge.

And this week, begin a *revolution* that will greatly impact your world & make it a better place to be!

Ready?

Charge!

Reflections for Week 51 . . .

Tough love is a very popular phrase – how about revolutionary love – undeniable love. Love really is dimensional, multi—faceted like a kaleidoscope.

Is the concept of loving, of being soft, robbing us of the other dimensions of love?

What other dimensions of love do you want to grow in?

Exercise more?

When others act in those bold ways, does that threaten you?

Do you see it as their acts of bold love?

Do you allow the people around you to love boldly or do you try to quiet them?

With whom do you need to express these other dimensions of love?

Your Reflections Week 51 . . .

WEEK 52: CHOOSE LOVE ~

Against all odds!

The human spirit can survive insurmountable odds! The human spirit is made of and from LOVE!

This fact was driven home to me as I read the report of the Chilean miners rescue a year or so ago. Men who, one by one - after 69 days a half-mile underground, rose from a black pit with happy smiling faces. As I embraced their joy via TV, I realized that we too can overcome the "humanly impossible!"

Today, if life meets you with a mountain you're sure you can't climb; think again. LOVE says you can! Take a deep breath, whisper a quiet prayer and then take that first step.

Organize your thoughts & summon up energy you never thought you had. Suddenly, the mountain doesn't seem so large after all.

Wisdom for the week! Believe you can. Believe you will.

Then take the 1st step in the direction of - "I did!"

Reflections for Week 52 . . .

Love, the motivator.

There are many stories, when in adversity, someone said it was the love of, or for someone that kept them going....that helped them survive!

Have you ever considered love as a motivator - beyond just the traditional sense?

How about love as a motivator in your professional success?

Dealing with an unruly boss?

Finishing a less than desirable project?

Or with the routine chores we might seldom think of with loving motivation?

Cleaning house?

Reading a book?

What are some unusual areas in which you could use love as a motivator?

Your Reflections Week 52 . . .

TO A NEW DAY ~ A NEW WEEK ~ A NEW YEAR!

Are you a "steel magnolia"?

A woman with a backbone made of metal. One who can weather any storm life brings you?

My suspicion is that each of you is such a woman. One who can stand tall against the winds of time!

In fact, I'm quite sure of it!

Thus, as you complete a year's worth of 'LOVE NOTES', let me encourage you to celebrate your strength, courage and tenacity!

Whatever may be part of life for you now, you can manage it.

So lift your head high and move forward knowing that nothing - but nothing - can stand in your way or bow you over.

There - I said it!

Believe it, for it is absolutely TRUE!

EPILOGUE ~

Prepare to Be

Remember the story about the woman with the "critical need"?

The woman who persevered against all odds to reach from out the crowd just to touch the hem of the man's garment? The woman who so desperately wanted to be healed and made whole? The woman who would not be deterred from the task at hand?

A woman who believed against all odds – that one touch would be just what she needed to be whole again!

That event was eons ago; recorded for all of us to ponder as we seek the same healing and wholeness.

Our 'issue' may not be that of the woman in the story; but each of us has a life 'issue' of which we need healing and a return to wholeness!

Our challenge is several fold:

1). To recognize & readily admit we have such an 'issue',

2). To admit we have a need to be 'healed' - of anything in our lives,

3). To take the bold step of reaching out against the odds that keep us standing amidst the crowd of life's daily tasks,

4). To have the faith it takes to believe 'reaching out' will accomplish our desired outcome(s),

5). And, to s-t-r-e-t-c-h ourselves beyond what we think is humanly possible, to accomplish the desired ends we so long to achieve.

I challenge you to look back at the last 52 weeks of LOVE NOTES that hopefully you have worked with and through; to find any "issues" that remain bleeding, open wounds – wounds crying out for health, wellness and wholeness!

Yes, I am lovingly throwing 'down the gauntlet'. Lovingly laying before you the challenge.

The question remains – will you pick it up?

Will you take up the challenge and s-t-r-e-t-c-h, against all that looms as obstacles in the path, to make health and wholeness yours?

Ultimately, the choice is yours!

JoAnn and I have given you the tools.

Using them to achieve one more step on your path to greatness is - in your hands. . .

Warmly,

Linda & JoAnn . . .

ABOUT THE AUTHORS . . .

LINDA S. FITZGERALD ~ Linda is CEO and chief visionary officer for A Women's Place Network, Inc. doing business as Affiliated Women International™ (AWI). She writes and speaks to the hearts of women with a passion to see each of them fulfill their ultimate destiny and achieve the fulfillment of their dreams and desires.

Linda is a mentor and coach who daily seeks to add value to the lives of the women she calls 'family' through the organization's online community at http://affiliatedwomenlive.com and face-to-face AWI Neighborhood Networks™ across North America. She recently launched *"Successful Life Strategies"*, a year-long mentoring program for mid-life women seeking personal - professional growth!

Her career in counseling and organizational development spans over 30 years with program development in the health care industry, fund raising development, early care and education and creative business development. Linda is also the author of a children's book: "Stellar the Teeniest, Tiniest Star in the Universe".

Linda lives in 'East Central Indiana with long-time friend Harold and near her daughters and six grandchildren. She will soon become a great-grandmom for the first time!

JOANN CORLEY ~ JoAnn Corley is a dynamic, inspiring speaker, trainer, career and management coach. She has a contagious passion and energy for the topics she teaches and has shared that passion with thousands across North America specializing in seminars on Getting Results, Creative and Innovative Thinking, Emotional Intelligence, Effective Management and Leadership, Powerful Communication and Team Collaboration. You can find out more about her seminars here: www.joanncorley.com.

She is author of several books and creator of the newly launched employee training app – The 1% Edge Portable coach available on all smartphone platforms. Her most recent book release is Organizational Strategies for the Overwhelmed, How to Manage Your Time, Space, & Priorities to Work Smart, Get Results, & Be Happy. She is also contributing author to the book, Ordinary Women, Extraordinary Success, a collaborative effort with some of the top female motivational speakers in North American and hailed by Jack Canfield of Chicken Soup for the Soul fame as a must read.

Companies whose employees have experienced JoAnn's dynamic workshops include: The City of Chicago, U.S. Marshals Service, Microsoft, 3M Corporation, Trump Enterprises, NASA,

University of Texas, and the U.S. Army, Fort Hood, TX, The Chicago White Soxs, Duke University, The Yale Club of New York City, HBO, & ESPN to name a few.

What Others Have to Say. . .

"A year's worth of love notes to send to myself - what a wise investment. This is wonderful!"

Sue Savage, PhD LCPC, Co-author Dream, Dare, Dance

"In our fast paced world, taking time to reflect on life is so very important for our spiritual, mental and physical well-being. This book is a wonderful resource of heartfelt wisdom, delivered innovatively with reflective exercises that will accelerate your personal success. Don't just read this book; reflect, reflect, reflect!"

Dave Carpenter, Mentor to the Stars

www.accelerate-success.com

"Love Notes of the Heart" truly is of the heart! Filled with insight and wisdom designed to not only help you know yourself more fully but to love yourself more fully. I not only enjoyed reading it, I felt the impact immediately from doing the reflections with the first week and it just keeps getting deeper. It is more than a book, it is written for you and by you! A companion guide to living a richer life every day; read it, write it, use it - there is so much to gain from it!

Tap into the juice of life!!!

Edie Galley, Sales Growth & Development Coach

"Thought Leader for Courageous Living"

"Love Notes" is a working journal which provokes self-discovery. It makes you think. Use this journal to nurture yourself and create balance in your life. Through your reflections, you will re-examine many areas of your life, which will assist you in enhancing your relationships, choosing a new path, and once again finding the "magic" of a healthy self-esteem.

Judi Moreo, Author, "You Are More Than Enough"

www.ingramcontent.com/pod-product-compliance
Lightning Source LLC
Chambersburg PA
CBHW081148270326
41930CB00014B/3082

* 9 7 8 0 6 1 5 6 6 6 0 2 0 *